WRITING PARAGRAPHS WORKBOOK

I0133229

How to Make Your Writing Great!

HERON BOOKS
K-12 CURRICULUM

Published by
Heron Books, Inc.
20950 SW Rock Creek Road
Sheridan, OR 97378

heronbooks.com

First Edition © 2019, Heron Books
All Rights Reserved

ISBN: 0-89739-151-9

Printed in the USA

10 July 2019

In This Book

This book belongs to:

Activity 1
Nouns and Verbs

Label the nouns and verbs in these sentences. You can use *n* for noun and *v* for verb.

           n   **n**   **n**   **v**

Example: The dog in my neighbor's yard is barking.

The girl walked to the store.

George jumped over the fence.

My friends will visit tomorrow.

Our dog will be happy in our new house.

The road was covered with leaves.

My sister will become a dancer.

Janelle will play soccer tomorrow.

My uncle has a new car.

The kids walked to school together.

That lion looks fierce.

Funny Sentences with Nouns and Verbs

Use these nouns and verbs to make as many funny sentences as you can. You can add a few more nouns or verbs if you like.

NOUNS	VERBS
turtle	talks
arrow	jumps
phone	flies
school	is

Activity 3
Find the Adjectives

Find the nouns and adjectives in each sentence and notice which noun is being described by an adjective.

Label the nouns and adjectives. You can use *n* for noun and *adj* for adjective.

Example: The black dog chased a big cat up the tree.

Susan's teacher gave her a long assignment.

Spicy peppers burn my tongue.

Look at the purple and white kites in the sky!

The tired carpenter took a break.

The mailman carried the heavy bag.

A fat, sleepy dog is snoozing on the mat.

Samir baked a huge pie.

My favorite movie won an award!

The beautiful baby smiled at her father.

Activity 4
Add the Adjectives

Fill in an adjective to tell more about the noun in each sentence. You can make them as silly or as serious as you like.

Example: I had <u>squishy</u> cake for my party.

The _____ sun at the beach was nice.

The wind was _____.

Did you see the _____ elephant?

We danced to the _____ music.

My cat is too _____ to hunt.

That joke is _____!

I counted _____ squirrels in my yard.

My aunt grows _____ roses.

Adverbs with Verbs

Find the verb in each sentence. Notice the adverb that tells more about the verb.

Label the verbs and adverbs. You can use *v* for verb and *adv* for adverb.

v   adv

Example: Ten birds sang yesterday in a tree.

A squirrel quickly climbed the tree.

The lightning flashed brightly in the sky.

A frog suddenly hopped out of the bush.

Joan tiptoed quietly down the stairs.

Cows munch contentedly on the grass.

The tree grew slowly in my yard.

She knits better than I do.

A bird is singing beautifully.

Activity 6
Adverbs with Adjectives

Find the adjective in each sentence. Notice the adverb that tells more about the adjective. Hint: not every adjective has an adverb.

Label the adjectives and adverbs in these sentences. You can use *adj* for adjective and *adv* for adverb.

>   **adv adj**
> **Example: We played very loud music at the picnic.**

I saw a dark red car speed down the street.

Sandra painted a very nice picture for the art show.

That bird has sparkly blue feathers.

Jaylin brought his super crazy dog to my house!

There was a dusty brown lion napping in the grass.

I was the most excited person at the circus.

My kitten is so funny!

My mom bought light green apples for the pie.

Activity 7
Adverbs with Adverbs

Find the adverbs in these sentences. Notice which adverb is telling more about another adverb.

Label the adverbs in these sentences. You can use *adv* for adverb.

        adv   adv
Example: I waited very patiently for the cookies to be baked.

Kelly coughed extremely loudly.

Jackson very quickly hid the cookies.

The rain fell super hard today.

My dog runs more slowly than my cat.

I sang extra loudly last night.

Carry that glass bowl extra carefully.

Asad almost never leaves early.

My team played so well today!

Activity 8
Add the Adverbs

Add adverbs to these sentences. Try not to use *really* or *very* more than once each.

Adverbs with Verbs

Kelly sang _____ .

Jen _____ placed the egg on the table.

The parade went _____ down the street.

I packed _____ for the trip.

Adverbs with Adjectives

The rose is _____ red.

We played _____ loud music at the cookout.

Lia is _____ worried than he was yesterday.

That pig is _____ fat than he was before!

Adverbs with Adverbs

The man spoke _____ politely to me.

We _____ seldom see zebras here.

I _____ always have cake for my birthday.

The boy ran _____ quickly and fell down.

Activity 9
Articles

Underline the articles in these sentences.

Example: I found <u>a</u> really slimy worm under <u>the</u> rock.

The gardener needs a bigger shovel.

I would like a tall lemonade to go with the pie I am eating.

Can we get an orange, a lemon and an avocado?

I really didn't like the movie I saw yesterday.

The dog dug an extremely large hole in the yard.

We won't need the tent at the beach but we will need a blanket.

Fill in each blank with *a* or *an*.

Can I have _____ ice cream sundae please?

I want _____ cookie with chocolate chips.

Would you like _____ banana?

Did you see _____ orangutan at the zoo?

It took us _____ hour to drive home today!

We found _____ great present for my dad.

Activity 10
Use the Words!

Write at least six sentences that use nouns, verbs, adjectives, adverbs and articles. You don't have to use all five kinds of words in each sentence.

Label your sentences to show each noun, verb, adjective, adverb or article.

          n   v   v   art   n   v   art   n
Example: Lin is looking out the window watching the rain.

Activity 11
Find the Pronouns

he	me	they	her	she	you
it	us	I	we	him	them

Underline the pronouns in these sentences.

Example: <u>They</u> gave <u>me</u> a really nice gift.

He is one of my best friends.

Can we come see you later today?

Please give me the book.

Will you play with us later?

I think she will be here soon.

I told them to be here by noon but they are late.

You and I can pick apples and make a pie.

Sia and Ben said we could go to the play with them.

13

Activity 12
Add the Pronouns

Cross out the underlined nouns and replace them with pronouns.

he	me	they	she	you	it
us	I	we	him	them	

Example: <del>Sally</del> really likes chocolate cake.
       She

Hi! My name is Jake. Let <u>Jake</u> tell you a story about my friends, Leo and Bess.

Last week <u>Leo and Bess and Jake</u> went fishing. Leo packed a big lunch for when <u>Leo and Bess and Jake</u> got hungry. <u>Leo</u> wanted to eat the lunch early in the day. <u>Bess</u> wanted to eat <u>the lunch</u> later. <u>Leo and Bess</u> got into a huge argument about <u>the lunch</u>.

Jake told <u>Leo and Bess</u> to calm down but <u>Leo and Bess</u> kept arguing. While Leo and Bess were arguing <u>Jake</u> got hungry. <u>Jake</u> ended up eating all the lunch. <u>Leo and Bess</u> were furious!

Find the Conjunctions

and	but	or	because

Underline the conjunctions in these sentences.

Example: I can play violin <u>and</u> piano.

I went to the beach and the river last summer.

Addy can't decide if she wants blue or green for her room.

Jae won't be able to come to school because he is sick.

I would really like to come to the party but I will be on vacation then.

We tried to close the door because it was raining but we couldn't.

I would like the apple and the orange but not the pineapple.

Should we have pretzels or potato chips for snack?

Red and blue are my favorite colors but my sister likes green.

Activity 14
Using Conjunctions

Combine the sentences using one of these conjunctions. Underline the conjunction.

and	but	or	because

Example: We went to the circus. We went to the park.
We went to the circus <u>and</u> the park.

I am hiding in the closet. There is a thunderstorm.

_____

_____

She wants to play baseball. She wants to play soccer.

_____

_____

My mom said we might go to the beach. We had too much work to do.

_____

_____

Would you like lemonade? Would you like water?

_____

_____

Activity 15
Find the Prepositions

Underline the prepositions in these sentences.

Example: My dog is hiding <u>under</u> the bed.

I put the basket on the table and the box behind the door.

My mother doesn't like anything hidden on top of the cabinet.

We tried to run between the raindrops but we got wet anyway.

Look through my books and see which ones you like.

The dog barked during the night.

The cat jumped onto the dog and scared him.

We can't go shopping without money!

I live in the red house next to the park.

Activity 16
Add Prepositions

Add a preposition to complete each sentence. You can use the list of prepositions in the *Writing Paragraphs* book for ideas.

Example: By mistake I went to the store <u>without</u> any money.

I planted daisies _____ the tree.

Ty did the dishes _____ he did his homework.

Will you please walk the dog _____ dinner?

Don't keep the horse _____ the barn on a nice day.

Please put your bike _____ the house.

My cats like to sleep _____ each other.

My dad likes to eat jelly _____ peanut butter.

My paper airplane crashed _____ the wall.

Activity 17
Interjections

Write down as many interjections as you can think of (you don't have to use all the lines).

_____   _____

_____   _____

_____   _____

Write a sentence using each interjection you thought of.

_____

_____

_____

_____

_____

_____

_____

_____

Activity 18
Find the Subjects

Draw a line under the subject of each sentence.

Example: <u>The tree</u> is very tall.

The old tree shook its leaves angrily.

At the zoo, the monkey was my favorite animal.

Along the road, oak trees are growing.

Elephants, giraffes, seals and eagles can be seen at the zoo.

My sister and I are always playing.

After playing in the rain, my dog was muddy and tired.

John, Joe and Susie were late today.

The lizard with the long tongue and the green and white spots is pretty.

Before breakfast, my sister and I went out to make snowmen.

Mario's family and Bill's family live near each other.

Find the Subjects in Questions

Draw a line under the subject of each question.

Where is the dog?

Did the bus already leave?

Are the dog and cat supposed to be fighting?

Does he know?

When did the girl and her dog leave for the hike?

How in the world did this get here?

What did John find in the scary old house?

Can you hear the frogs croaking?

Activity 20
Write Sentences

Write the following sentences. Underline the subject in each one:

Write a two-word sentence.

_____

Write a three-word question.

_____

Write a five-word sentence.

_____

_____

Write a long sentence of ten words or more.

_____

_____

Write a long question.

_____

_____

_____

Activity 21
Complete or Incomplete?

1. Mark each complete sentence or question with a *C* and each incomplete sentence with an *I*. Put the correct punctuation at the end of each complete sentence or question.

   My sister went to school

   If I could go to school

   When we studied math, we learned to multiply

   Jason and Allison are going to the movies together

   Whenever I watch movies

   Since I graduated

   What are you eating

2. Complete the incomplete sentences you marked above.

Activity 22

Find the Main Thoughts

1. Underline each main thought in this run-on sentence. Then write it over using complete sentences. You can change some words so the sentences make sense if you need to.

After I got on the school bus, I sat down next to the red-haired girl but she was reading her book and ignored me, so I got out my lunch and started eating it, so when I got to school I didn't have enough left for lunch and the teacher had me call my mother who said she would bring more food, but she didn't get there until too late, and I ended up being hungry anyway.

Fix a Run-on Sentence

1. Write a long run-on sentence with several main thoughts. Then break up your run-on sentence into shorter sentences that are complete. Be sure each part is now a complete sentence.

www.ingramcontent.com/pod-product-compliance
Lightning Source LLC
Chambersburg PA
CBHW081012040426
42443CB00016B/3496